Ministe

Integrity

in Liturgy

by
Charles H. Hutchins
Team Rector, Kingswood Team Ministry, Bristol

GROVE BOOKS LIMITED
Bramcote   Nottingham   NG9 3DS

CONTENTS

ACKNOWLEDGMENTS

My thanks to the members of the Group for the Renewal of Worship whose fellowship and stimulating comments are a constant encouragement. To my colleague Rob Martin and my wife Leta, who read the draft and made valuable comments and corrections; and to my secretary Kate Gillman who patiently worked on the word processor, my grateful thanks.

CHH June 1993

THE COVER PICTURE

is by Paul Ellis

First Impressions July 1993

ISSN 0305-3067

ISBN 1 85174 240 9

INTRODUCTION

What is in store in ministry? For the aspiring person feeling called towards the full-time ordained ministry there is always the wonder as to what it will be like; the excitement of the possibilities of divine grace in the lives of individuals; the prospect of a hard life with demands on time which, if the minister is a family person, will often precipitate conflicts of loyalty to God, family and 'work'. Usually the minister will already have had to work out Christian principles in daily life through previous employment, but ministry makes it a lot more public and 'doing the Lord's work' can lead to neglect of the family.

The question of integrity is one which faces every Christian called to be a disciple in the market place. Nothing is as cut and dried as we might like, even in the Bible itself, and there are doubtful areas where some dedicated Christians would opt out and object, whilst others would stay put and work for change. The principles upon which some businesses prosper are rightly challenged, and the action some Christians call for does not always meet with widespread agreement. There are varying stances over Sabbath keeping, Sunday trading, the place of television, censorship—the list is endless (see the Grove Ethics series).[1]

In ministry and pew there are a number of areas where integrity is challenged and whilst it is all part and parcel of the rich and fulfilling response to the Lord's command to go and make disciples, many ministers and lay people are in danger of being worn down by conflicts of people's demands[2] which are not always gospel demands where integrity is challenged. It is those areas which I attempt to draw together.

But what is integrity? Definitions include:
1. Adherence to moral principles, honesty
2. The quality of being unimpaired
3. Unity, wholeness

In day by day living we all know instinctively when someone is not being straight, true or honest. The TV camera picks it up, and personal encounter soon enables us to know when someone is being unscrupulous or unprincipled; children are upset when there is lack of consistency in action.

Our concern in this enquiry is the place of integrity in the life of the church where liturgy impinges on pastoral activity. At first sight it might be thought to affect only ministers, and some of the cries when a minister calls for a more stringent approach on a subject imply this, but their opposers allege that it is only for the sake of their own conscience that such a course of action is demanded. In reality the question of integrity is wider than that. Lay people as well as ordained are affected, as we know when congregational members disturb the waters and express their surprise at liturgical events and their participants. Indeed it is very often the 'unlikely' people who seek blessings on new rings, prayer at significant times in their life, or attend the Midnight Mass in adultery, event causing 'ordinary' church members to raise their eyebrows supposing the minister/vicar has been 'compromised'.

---

[1] Grove Ethical Studies Series has now reached no. 90 so there is no shortage of issues.
[2] Pete Meadows *Pressure Points*—especially his chapter on 'The world and the church on my back'.

Questions about integrity arise mainly through the Occasional Offices—Baptism, Marriage and Funerals—and the problem is often compounded because emotional reactions personalize matters. Questions also arise where there are civic demands and inter-faith issues. It is around these various issues in contrasting contexts that we explore integrity.

In the NIV there are 22 references to integrity.[1]

[1] Deuteronomy 9.5 'It is not because of your righteousness or your integrity that you are going in to take possession of their land; but on account of the wickedness of these nations, the LORD your God will drive them out before you, to accomplish what he swore to your fathers, to Abraham, Isaac and Jacob.'

I Kings 9.4 'As for you, if you walk before me in integrity of heart and uprightness, as David your father did, and do all I command and observe my decrees and laws.'

I Chronicles 29.17 'I know, my God, that you test the heart and are pleased with integrity. All these things have I given willingly and with honest intent. And now I have seen with joy how willingly your people who are here have given to you.'

Nehemiah 7.2 'I put in charge of Jerusalem my brother Hanani, along with Hananiah the commander of the citadel, because he was a man of integrity and feared God more than most men do.'

Job 2.3 'Then the LORD said to Satan, "Have you considered my servant Job? There is no one on earth like him; he is blameless and upright, a man who fears God and shuns evil. And he still maintains his integrity, though you incited me against him to ruin him without any reason." '

Job 2.9 'His wife said to him, "Are you still holding on to your integrity? Curse God and die!" '

Job 6.29 'Relent, do not be unjust; reconsider, for my integrity is at stake.'

Job 27.5 'I will never admit you are in the right; till I die, I will not deny my integrity.'

Psalms 7.8 'Let the LORD judge the peoples. Judge me, O LORD, according to my righteousness, according to my integrity, O Most High.'

Psalm 25.21 'May integrity and uprightness protect me, because my hope is in you.'

Psalm 41.12 'In my integrity you uphold me and set me in your presence forever.'

Psalm 78.72 'And David shepherded them with integrity of heart; with skilful hands he led them.'

Proverbs 10.9 'The man of integrity walks securely, but he who takes crooked paths will be found out.'

Proverbs 11.3 'The integrity of the upright guides them, but the unfaithful are destroyed by their duplicity.'

Proverbs 13.6 'Righteousness guards the man of integrity, but wickedness overthrows the sinner.'

Proverbs 17.26 'It is not good to punish an innocent man, or to flog officials for their integrity.'

Proverbs 29.10 'Bloodthirsty men hate a man of integrity and seek to kill the upright.'

Isaiah 45.23 'By myself I have sworn, my mouth has uttered in all integrity a word that will not be revoked. Before me every knee will bow; by me every tongue will swear.'

Isaiah 59.4 'No one calls for justice; no one pleads his case with integrity. They rely on empty arguments and speak lies; they conceive trouble and give birth to evil.'

Matthew 22.16 'They sent their disciples to him along with the Herodians. "Teacher," they said, "we know you are a man of integrity and that you teach the way of God in accordance with the truth. You aren't swayed by men, because you pay no attention to who they are." '

Mark 12.14 'They came to him and said, "Teacher, we know you are a man of integrity. You aren't swayed by men, because you pay no attention to who they are; but you teach the way of God in accordance with the truth. Is it right to pay taxes to Caesar or not?" '

Titus 2.7 'In everything set them an example by doing what is good. In your teaching show integrity. . .'

From these references we note six things.

1. *It is God's grace which is at work* (Deut. 9.5). God speaks clearly of the fact that no matter what our integrity and uprightness, the blessings are not earned or merited. Indeed it is the wickedness of others which brings about His action, not our integrity. That may help us to understand that in facing the questions and issues which come to us, we must never adopt any superior attitude over our action. Indeed, it should make us doubly humble and sensitive to people in their need.

2. *The challenge of integrity before God* (1 Kings 9.4 1; Chron. 29.17; Neh. 7.2; Psalm 7.8 and 25.21). God's desire and challenge is to measure ourselves, not against others, but against the holiness and purity of God himself.

3. *Integrity is an inner centre which is at peace whatever the externals* (Job 2.9, 6.29, 27.5; Matt. 22.16; Mark 12.14). Job stood firm and coped with the external circumstances and tragedy and the utter useless advice of friends. Inwardly, he may well have been torn apart but nonetheless, he appears to have had an inner centre which enabled him to stand firm. Even the Pharisees recognised that Jesus was not swayed by people.

4. *Through integrity people command respect* (Ps. 41.12; Ps. 78.72; Prov. 10.9, 11.3, 13.6). There is, despite the human condition, something which ultimately puts the consciences of others on the side of the person of integrity.

5. *But integrity does draw opposition* (Prov. 17.26, 29.10). Jesus drew opposition, ridicule and persecution, and the person of integrity never has an easy path. We need only to observe the national past-time of finding the feet of clay of leaders.

6. *Integrity is commanded* (Titus 2.7). Titus is told by Paul that he is to provide an example and with integrity to teach them.

To return to our dictionary definitions we see them illustrated from the biblical verses, viz. integrity is about being sound and without fault; it is about honesty and sticking to moral principles; and it is about wholeness.

So whose conscience are we to be concerned about? Is conscience entirely individual or is there a corporate dimension? Undoubtedly there are some clergy who are absolutely clear that there is but one dimension of conscience in the life of the church—that of the minister. Such clergy are found across the traditions and Protestant, Catholic and Liberals alike spawn them. Perhaps the humourless might be accused of making the greatest fuss over the smallest points, and certain personality types do appear to be drawn to particular theological positions, but the sad thing is that in those situations much hurt is engendered. Theological positions however strongly held, demand pastoral sensitivity. Integrity is not the minister's preserve.

In all difficult pastoral situations lay people also have aggrieved consciences and sometimes act as if no-one else can possibly have scruples. In some cases they want to dictate to minister, congregation and church alike the course of action to be followed. The sense of the body of Christ, of conscience having to be worked out in a corporate sense, is ignored. Ministers and lay people alike have issues of integrity. We have to ask where it pinches.

In some situations the matter is definitely a ministerial one. In others it will be for the whole congregation. In all circumstances the contrast and tension between perfection and reality; the ideal and the practicality, has to be measured and faced, however painful. The credibility gap is not a myth or an ivory tower question. The church before the watching world[1] is like the city on a hill which, according to Jesus, cannot be hid. The church and its ministers are expected to behave and act without impunity. Jesus teaches that we are to be perfect—an impossible ideal (Matt. 5.48) when we know our weaknesses and the reality of the world. But when we see his command as meaning 'being just right for the job', then we know that it is possible to fulfil our calling with integrity.

So those called and being called to the ordained ministry will find that, however exciting the life of ministry appears, living out matters of conscience in a goldfish bowl may not be as easy as was first imagined. Indeed it starts on the day of ordination when the preparations are completed. What are called the oaths of allegiance have to be made. Oaths of obedience to Queen and Bishop; the promise to use only authorized liturgical texts and to adopt a discipline of life. How seriously are the oaths taken, or expected to be taken? Now that assent to the 39 Articles is as a historic expression of the faith, it has made the oath easier rather than the tongue in cheek it had become for many. Once upon a time a mockery[2] if not a scandal was enacted, but the oaths to be taken at the start of ministry are but a foretaste of what might come! After all, the Bishop may have a style which is very directive, causing clergy and parishes to feel strait-jacketed and unable to act as they would prefer because they are aware of his views and have no desire to offend him.

[1] Francis Shaeffer, *The Church before the Watching World*
[2] Against Simony; of allegiance to Queen and to Bishop, and of using only services approved by Canon or the Ordinary.

1. WHAT ARE WE DOING IN LITURGY?

The leading of liturgy is the high profile part of the ministry now embarked upon. It is a skilled art which some learn well but others do not. The hidden agendas of spiritual life and expectation; the love of or hate of set liturgy; the mood of priest and people, all affect services. To lead a service is to drive a service and for priest, deacon and reader alike, indeed for any person leading liturgy it does need to be driven. There is a destination in view to which the participants are to be taken.[1]

Liturgy is also the high profile activity of the church in its corporate expression. It is the public image where committed and uncommitted, believer and sceptic confront the living expression of the unseen God revealed in Jesus Christ. Hence, what we are doing when we gather corporately is a question that needs to be implicit in all of our activity and at its least, it needs to be something which is done to the best of our ability to show what God is worth to us.

Despite liturgy's being such a high profile activity, those who are well experienced are tempted to turn up and do the job with minimal preparation. It is perhaps one of the dangers of having a set and provided liturgy, but preparation there must be. I remember a holiday when my wife and I visited a church on the Saturday evening to find out the times of the Sunday services and encountered the Vicar. He was of strong evangelical persuasion and made derogatory comments about a neighbouring church 'being evangelical with emphasis on the jelly'. But on the Sunday his was the one which showed up very badly. He forgot books and had to go back to the vestry; shuffled through papers throughout the service and led the worship in a perfunctory manner, whilst his neighbouring church to which we went in the evening, provided a well-ordered and well-prepared worship service. Another church of more catholic persuasion was not only chaotic in the ordering of things but there was a general tattiness with candle-wax and unkempt linen and furnishings. Integrity in preparation of worship and for preaching is important. Clergy and laity must beware of becoming negligent.

The task of getting the church ready, handing out hymn books, preparing the building, welcoming people, making sure microphones and other such modern technology is in proper working order and functioning properly, all these things, as in the theatre, have to be seen to before the curtain goes up. It is therefore a corporate activity and responsibility to make sure that what we are offering week by week, as worship, is the best. When we attend the theatre we have paid for the ticket and expect a professionalism consonant with the cost. The same should be true for worship. We have an appointment with the living God for public liturgy, and it is something for which all must take responsibility. Could low levels of giving be in any way affected by quality of worship?

Words and actions speak and they are inter-related. What is said; by whom they are said; what accompanying actions are used and seen. Some people get desperately upset if no hand is raised in blessing, or the

---

[1] See Colin Buchanan *Leading Worship* (Grove Worship Series 76).

sign of the cross is not made at absolution, or the manual acts are not used at the consecration/thanksgiving, or the elements are raised. In these situations ministers are faced with questions of integrity in terms of the local tradition and custom. Should the person be themselves and be true to their own thought-out theological convictions, or should they adopt practices to please/be sensitive to that congregation which is putting on constraints by expecting a particular ritual? What are ministers to do? Do they, for instance, elevate the elements against their own practice and theology, or refuse to against the local tradition? Or is the minister's own personal tradition to be forced on to a congregation no matter what their feelings and preferences? Serious pastoral breakdowns can come about through disputes over liturgy, which hit at the very heart of the life of the church. Because liturgy is the central corporate action, disputes can mean the loss of credibility before the watching world, if dirty linen gets washed in public.

When people gather together for worship there are many factors which affect the driving, performance and ethos. The type of building, whether traditional, ancient, modern; its temperature (how did former generations cope with the icy cold) and decor; the attitudes of the people present— expectation of God at work, or the ritual performance of tradition. The age and mix of the people present. All these factors are mixed up in terms of worship, alongside an understanding of the church as local, eclectic, separatist or parish. I have heard clergy speak in terms of 'letting those from the parish go elsewhere if they don't like what we do here', as well as lay people defending church premises, even though paid for by the local community as well as by church members, against use by outsiders.

This can become more complicated when groups of people take sides over the replacement or otherwise of a church building—even to sitting on opposite sides of the current meeting place, as reported recently by a visitor. Or when the charismatic versus non-charismatic; Prayer Book against ASB; new comers to a village against the die-hards; take posture and get into conflicting stances. Clergy standing in the middle of such tension may well find integrity stretched to the limit. The answer to the question as to whose church it is is simple—God's, but there is more to it than that! Indeed, the fact of being the established church with a population presuming they are Church of England, in itself causes tension over the ministrations of the church.

As far as people in general are concerned, with a population fast demoting and side-lining God, how they react to the Church building itself and treat it, not only says a great deal about them, but can put a minister in a difficult position and challenge integrity (perhaps unknowingly). At baptisms and at weddings, the traditional respect of quiet reverence no longer operates, as the abuse which can be encountered when videos and photographs are forbidden demonstrates. Yet the same people will respect without question prohibitions on videos and cameras in theatres and certainly no-one would be allowed into the religious buildings of other faiths without restrictions. Yet the Christian minister is expected and tempted to avoid offence and allow the church to be abused because of the weight of the pressure put on him.

There is no black and white ground, it is all grey, and many people who attend our churches for marriages and baptisms are ill at ease. But regular week by week worshippers also on occasion need a reminder of the purpose of worship. Time keeping is a favourite blind spot. People are still entering long after the appointed and publicised time. The visiting missioner who started the service at 6.30pm telling the Vicar who had only just appeared and was ready for a long chat that his appointment with God was at 6.30 and not later, made his point. Choir members still sitting talking when clergy arrive at the vestry; clergy arriving at the last minute; organists cutting it so fine that throughout the service there is activity for all to see as the organist seeks the right music. These are all areas where we can present worship as an important part of the church programme or trivialise it by behaviour. Where the Occasional Offices are concerned brides can be late and baptisms be delayed when attenders arrive late. Nonetheless, whilst we need to be sensitive in handling such situations, it has been my experience to find an innate gut reaction that 'we must get on with it' from those whose relatives have not appeared at the right and pre-arranged time. Music, important as it is for worship, is a great focus for concern in the liturgy. We know full well of the tensions caused in many churches, where a new and more modern hymn book has been introduced, or where a music group has supplemented or replaced the choir. These are issues which are part and parcel of the ongoing corporate life of the church but matters of integrity are raised when it comes to weddings and funerals if particular music is requested which is outside the normal church repertoire. Or it can affect regular worship also if music has to be photocopied and the overhead projector used and matters relating to copyright control and music licence are conveniently overlooked. Integrity must not be dictated to by convenience.[1]

In the choice of music, how wide a choice of music can be given without dishonouring God? Is pop music something which is acceptable for weddings, or indeed funerals? Football supporters who have been killed in a road crash and the relatives request 'You'll never walk alone'; Whitney Houston music for the bride to enter. One school of thought suggests that church music is something quite separate from secular music; another that music is music. But there is a line that has to be drawn somewhere. Where that line is drawn is one where integrity gets challenged. The pinch might come for clergy person, for organist, a choir member, or someone in the congregation. But the emotional dimension which affects the bride and her mother, or bereaved, or long standing traditionalists cannot be set aside lightly. In public worship, we are there to give praise to God. At a wedding, the liturgy is the celebration of two people getting married. At a funeral, giving thanks and affirming the Christian faith. Since these are all occasions when 'the Church is on show', no one, least of all the clergy, wants unpleasant repercussions undermining the occasion, due to a challenge over integrity.

[1] Music copyright address is: Christian Copyright Licencing Ltd, PO Box 1339, Eastbourne, East Sussex BN21 4YF.

2. BAPTISM

The young woman came to clergy 'surgery' at the appointed time to get a letter of permission for the baptism of her third child in a neighbouring parish. My colleague, responsible for the baptism policy, set about writing a letter. Meanwhile as I chatted to her it became apparent that she had an older child of Sunday School age. Did she attend? I enquired. The response and attitude prompted further discussion and it became clear that there was neither goodwill towards Sunday School, nor belief in the existence of God. It seems the desire to have the child baptized in the other parish and 'put on the roll there with the others in their family who had been done there' was an insurance policy against the day of resurrection! I would have found it difficult to sign the letter, but my colleague provided it. An interesting illustration in itself of different reactions!

Integrity! If there has been any area in my ministry which has caused me pain, it has been over baptism. I have no problems whatever with the theology of infant baptism, but the practice causes the pain. Seek to implement a requirement that godparents are all confirmed, and I discovered dishonesty as a matter of course in completing the forms. Integrity for parents was irrelevant. Where do you go then? Ask for evidence?! Or the question of preparation or none. The rigorist or the open approach at the end of the day still often leaves an element of doubt about whether parents and godparents mean the declarations they make, or whether they will jump through any hoop to get their child done.

And it is at this point the matters of integrity arise for both clergy and lay people. The clergy, feeling uncomfortable about apparent non-faith people presenting children for baptism want to salve their own consciences by making it hard—'at least I have fulfilled my duty' type of approach. Following the canonical directions about baptism being in a main service perhaps, they then discover, not necessarily a dropping off of requests because they have to stand up in the presence of the church congregation, but a reaction from the congregation itself who feel their integrity is at stake by the lack of evidence of regular worship from those presenting themselves for baptism.[1]

Who is to judge? Clearly God alone is the judge, and he knows the spiritual state of people, so we have no need nor right to judge. But yet we are called on to make decisions, and decisions can only be made on facts. And that will always demand integrity, for emotions can enter in and blur our judgments, and judgments made on only half-truths are avoided.

John Finney's recently published research survey *Finding Faith Today* is one of the most encouraging pieces of reading of late. Through it we realize that baptism and all that surrounds it is but one stage in the process towards faith. That being the case, to hold our integrity is important, whatever discipline we follow. But this process has its milestones.[2]

---

[1] Quote from a letter I received from a fellow clergyman.
  'The parish remains difficult because of . . . a small and influential group . . . We have had a major row over Baptisms being held at Parish Communion. I was told not to have any, contrary to Canon Law and best practice. There was much hostility and anger expressed by them at the last PCC because I would not back down'.
[2] John Finney, *Finding Faith Today* (Bible Society).

I remember the man who came to enquire about baptism for his daughter. He had come alone because, it transpired later, he did not want to put his wife through a rejection experience again. When I had said that of course our policy over baptism included baptizing children of second marriages, there was a visible sigh of joy, then it all poured out. He had come alone with gritted teeth because when, after his first marriage had failed and he and his new unmarried fiancée had wanted a church wedding, they had been rejected. Whether it was the rejection itself or the manner in which they felt it had happened I cannot judge, but now the willingness to baptize their child was a significant milestone in a process which led to regular worship. But other reactions occur. For instance at the close of a service during which we had baptized the child of a woman who had been in worship regularly over a few months, a young man asked to speak privately. It came as a shock to find he was basically objecting to the fact that his sister was having her child baptized. He had, he told me, been 'saved' a few months previously and could not understand why his sister 'who isn't a Christian' could have her child baptized, or why we would do it!

Traditionally the statement 'seeing this child is regenerate' was the pinch-point over integrity. Many felt it could not be said until the concept of categorical language was given higher profile in the 1970s, that is we speak theological truth in the service, not a series of hopes and might be's. But the problems of conscience are not only for the clergy, but for laity as well. When the Series 2 and then Series 3 services came in, congregations suddenly had all manner of problems over baptism. Baptisms during the main service meant the whole congregation was exposed to the challenge of welcoming the newly baptized children in a language they now understood, instead of the vagaries of 1662. Bonhoeffer's cheap and costly grace contrast was being highlighted in liturgical word and action.[1]

However, issues of baptism revolve not only around the integrity of clergy and their congregations, and the faith or otherwise of those seeking it, but also on parishes where a baptism policy is sought to be operated. There are parishes who do their own thing regardless of any Deanery or Diocesan arrangement and will accept any for baptism but they do nothing to provide instruction for those they accept. Clergy will often get squeezed into a mould of least resistance, and, in their wanting to bring people to faith rather than put them off, that is not surprising. The problem is always the question of judgment as to whether a stricter rather than a more lenient path is likely to lead that way. In reality I could illustrate both approaches successfully. The sacrament is God's and it his grace which saves people.

Today's moral climate and economic structure means that we have an increasing number of single-parent families and more and more people are living together prior to marriage, with a significant proportion having children before marriage. Whilst it is clear that children must not be penalized when it comes to making the baptismal promises as they would for confirmation, then questions of integrity and conscience arise. Does renunciation of evil include not living together before marriage? The rub comes not in high-level statements of synods or even bishops but in week-by-week pastoral care and encounter with people.

[1] Bonhoeffer *The Cost of Discipleship* (SCM)

3. MARRIAGE

There are interesting contrasts of attitudes surrounding church weddings. There are Christians who would be happier if their own non practising children did not 'misuse' the church by getting married there; there are Christians who believe marriage in church should be only for practising church members; there are pagans who would go to the highest legal body if they could not get their own way for a church wedding; there are non-Christians who allege it is a great act of hypocrisy on the part of certain people who desire church weddings. Integrity does not have an easy ride. Some would say that the church is being taken for a ride; some would argue for the gospel opportunities weddings provide; but the sharp end is felt by the clergy person meeting the demands of enquirers and by the lay people listening to the comments of work-mates and neighbours.

What standing or status is the church to have before the watching world? The church is certainly constantly in the public eye and when it keeps quiet there are those who would have hoped it had spoken out or acted; if it speaks out, they wish it had remained silent. The church is seen by those outside it as at once irrelevant and indispensable. The church's own self-perception is therefore important. How is the church to order its life in relation to its dealings with the public? Is the church to be ready and willing to be the servant, at everybody's beck and call, setting no boundaries and having no discipline, or is the church to be concerned for her reputation, holiness and witness? One of the marks of the church for the Reformers was discipline.[1]

There are churches and clergy who will bend the rules and regulations in order to accommodate a given situation. One clergyman for instance, staged weddings at 'his' church at half-hour intervals and would not assign his fees to the diocese, so that he could increase his income by well over £1,000 a year above the diocesan stipend. But that was complicated even further because not all the weddings were those of parishioners, but of people from anywhere around whom he would put on the Electoral Roll without a requirement of attendance at worship. Only recently someone being married in a church other than where they both lived declared that it was possible because they had been put on the 'Electric Roll' of that church!! So we might ask who was taking whom for a ride? Where was integrity in all this? Did the congregation know? How did they feel about it?

On the other hand there are situations where the public in general cannot understand any demand being made and there is a complete lack of understanding of the legal requirements when they are being implemented. In today's moral climate, it would seem that any idea of rules being rules and therefore to be observed, is a foreign concept. The fact that Anglican clergy act as registrars means they have to observe the law, which is outside of them and which they simply administer. Yet we find members of the public expecting the clergy person to bend the law for their benefit in a way they would not expect the registrar at the Registry Office to do. Clergy thereby have their integrity tested.

[1] See Philip Hughes *The Theology of the English Reformers* (Hodder) ch viii; also Article 19.

The parochial system of residence and its legalities causes hurt when a Special Licence is proposed rather than our accepting nominal or fictitious membership of the Electoral Roll, or address. Banns are the usual required preparation for the ceremony, but truth over living abode is at some times strange. Clearly, truth does cause pain and a couple who, having made their wedding arrangements quite legitimately two years previously, think the clergy are being moralistic when now having moved out of the parish to live together, they interpret the suggestion of a special licence as a judgment on their morality rather than legal requirements.

Then there is the question of the re-marriage of those who have been divorced. There are three possible answers to enquirers.[1] One is blank refusal, another is blanket acceptance, the third is to judge every application separately and to enter the arena of pain where accusations of inconsistency and favouritism will be made (especially in close-knit communities such as villages, where often the clergy person knows least, having come in from outside, and where the long standing church members are not prepared to make the decision for fear of being alienated by the local community). Whose conscience is then being safeguarded or hurt, is not a straightforward conclusion. Integrity is not necessarily being upheld by a blanket refusal. Those who take that stance will often plead that it is not easy to refuse, but in reality it can be a soft option, hiding behind some principle given by or taken from some authority, be it Bible or Bishop. Nor is integrity necessarily being safeguarded by acceptance, for the couple themselves might have knowledge which they have not imparted.

Churches and ministers who are willing to conduct marriage ceremonies for divorced people may or may not believe they take the hardest and Biblical route, but there are pitfalls for them as well. The 'innocent' partner in one instance went to a minister to relate in a state of anguish the fact that her husband had walked out on her after a matter of months and gone off with another woman. After two years he had got a divorce, and now, she had heard, he was getting married again to yet another woman in the minister's church, and he was not yet 25. How integrity can be safeguarded is hard to know. Whether insufficient enquiry had been made in the first place by the clergy or whether more arbitrary rules need to be introduced is debatable. For example, no re-marriage if you are still under thirty, or not until more than two years have elapsed after the decree absolute has been granted. But then is not that the path which leads to the one followed by the Pharisees all those years ago who sought to safeguard God and lost him behind burdens unable to be borne?

Marriage may well be an Occasional Office with great evangelistic opportunity, but it is also an area which demands patient preparation and offers great scope for misunderstandings! The church which takes marriage preparations seriously, often finds that the couples themselves are hesitant, embarrassed, or even rebellious over invitations to attend marriage preparations. There are couples who are concerned only for the setting of photographs in choosing a church, or even whether a video recording is allowed or not. All these matters are a constant hassle for the clergyman, or Parish Office.

[1] Robert Warren *Divorce and Re-marriage* (Grove Pastoral 51); see also Gary Jenkins *Cohabitation: a Biblical Perspective* (Grove Ethical Studies 84) and Greg Forster *Marriage before Marriage?* (Grove Ethical Studies 69).

4. FUNERALS

It is Wednesday lunch-time and the telephone rings. 'Good morning vicar, can you help us please? We have a funeral come in for Monday morning and the daughter of the deceased has specifically asked for you because you married her back in the beginning of the year'.

'Let's have a look and see what the diary's like. Yes, that's okay' and the details are given and that is how it is left by the funeral director.

I make a telephone call and I go and see her. Pressure on the diary is quite heavy, since between now and Monday I have a day conference, a day off and Sunday duties, so despite the fact she is feeling sore from the sudden bereavement and I would prefer to see her again later, she is quite happy to sit and talk and I am able to minister to her.

The significant point in this visit was an aside. 'Oh, by the way, he was a member of the Buffs and they want to do something at the funeral'. 'The Buffs' means the Royal Antediluvian Order of Buffalos, Grand Lodge of England. I tell her that if they are intending to do something it will be after I have finished and I will go out from the Chapel. 'Oh no, there's no need for you to go out' she says 'you stay in. You will be most welcome.' But I know this is going to be difficult and I leave it at that point. It is not the time to get involved in debate and conflict, sensitive pastoral care is needed.

She phones me on the Saturday morning to confirm that indeed the Buffs are going to do something at the funeral and I also affirm the fact that they will do whatever they want to do *after* I have finished. I had decided to accommodate rather than cause conflict and hurt by refusal, but it had to be on my terms. This meant I would leave them to do their thing after I had finished and go to the back of the chapel making the contrast clear.

It was the ethos, as well as the words of what followed that made me feel sad. I was glad that I had done the service first and that there had been a positive, audible and confident service, giving thanks to God for a man who had not been a practising Christian in later years but had clearly been involved in church life in earlier ones. For what followed was half a dozen of the Buffalo Lodge gathering around the catafalque, linking hands, except with a gap where his death had broken the chain; and the person reading the service did so in an uninspiring and almost inaudible way.

The words used were devoid of any mention of Jesus Christ and phrases like 'we go from one design to another, adding hope to hope wrapped up in the contemplation of our worldly advancement' and 'passed to the glory of the light beyond'. 'Each break in the link demonstrates only too vividly the certainty of that end, towards which we are all hastening' were the substance of the observance. It seemed but a pale reflection of anything the Christian funeral service would want to say.

But it was the reference to the Grand Lodge above which begged some theological issues—'May we be firm and consistent in the practice of the principles of our Honourable Order and when in God's good time we are called to join the link in the Grand Lodge above, may we leave behind sweet and fragrant memories which we cherished beyond the grave.' If one had had the opportunity to speak after, was an immediate feeling, but one could only pray that the earlier Christian service had spoken to some heart. It was a stark reminder that the level of Christian understanding is so low that the need for gospel teaching is paramount in pastoral care and follow up. Theological integrity is not easy as any examining folk religion recognizes.[1]

It was noticeable in this instance that the funeral marshall and those around him did not join in the Christian service (ASB), nor join in the singing of the hymn. They had appeared off hand in speaking to me alleging that the family had asked for a Buffalo funeral but it is of course in these times of grief and bereavement that confrontation is the most difficult course to take. I had been given two pictures—on the one hand from the family that the Buffs wanted to do something and now from the Buffs that the family wanted them to do something.

Widening our concern to funerals in general, we move on to the place of a eulogy about the deceased. In many instances the Anglican clergy will not even have met the person but a cold raw lack of mention is hardly helpful to anyone. Hence most clergy develop the skill of putting in a nutshell a word picture summary of a person and in many cases families will provide the written script. The Roman Catholic church precludes any eulogy in its funeral service. The intention being to affirm the Christian gospel and certainly, in some situations, that might feel a very safe rubric behind which to hide. But there are other ways of dealing with it because there are occasions when a member of the family wishes to say something about the deceased and when this happens, the minister is then left completely free to make a statement about the gospel. Perhaps in times past, there was a greater desire to hold memorial services some time after the funeral service itself but with the absence of a memorial service, it is inevitable that at the funeral service there is a bringing together of memory and liturgy. If there were to be a memorial service some time after the funeral service, that would be the obvious place for a eulogy but as it is, somehow there does appear to be the need to incorporate both themes into the one service. Of course this is not always easy at a crematorium, when one is allowed only 15 minutes. In those situations, we really do rub up against a completely secular approach to death. Something which is clinical and speedy—it is no wonder that many people find the grieving process difficult to cope with. Our society, being the fast moving society that it is, wants to get things over and done with as quickly as possible and life to revert to its former pattern. But it doesn't.

With the increasing secularism in society the question of conscience over some funerals is gradually being removed as the humanist society provide people to conduct funerals and there seems to be a growing market for their trade. At least this gets over the dishonesty illustrated by the following. One widow when asked whether her husband was a Christian answered 'No, he was Church of England.' Another minister found himself requested to conduct a funeral where the family wanted all references

[1] See Chris Sugden *The Natural Mystery of Folk Religion* (Grove Spirituality 43)

to the resurrection to be deleted. Here was a true pricking point. Their honesty was clear, but what should the minister do? I understand he acceded to their request.

What if the deceased has been a rogue and a rotter? What does the minister do when asked not to refer to those facts? We must all stand before the judgment seat of Christ the funeral service tells us, so how do we square the words with what is known by the mourners present of the lifestyle of the deceased? Here we enter the eschatological dimension. What theology do we hold as people conducting funerals regarding the afterlife? How do we apply that theology in the service with pastoral care, for clearly it would be the most insensitive of people who would state publicly that the deceased was going to hell! But equally, can we make the opposite assertion of comfort and certainty if there is genuine doubt? The way forward must be to speak in objective terms as to the gospel position and leave people to make conclusions for themselves.

When ministering to the bereaved and visiting relatives in preparation for the funeral, a minister may well find that only one part or member of the family is present. This is especially so when there has been divorce and remarriage. Perhaps, as happened to me once. I was dealing with the widow and in visiting her it was only as I was bringing the discussion to a close, having gained the information that I needed, that I realised that I was in fact speaking to a widow who had been married to the man for only three years, whilst his daughter of 50 had been excluded. Clergy often find themselves in the reconciling and mediating position and get torn and hurt in the process. Tony Walter asks the question. 'How were we all to commemorate my father's life with integrity? Can a religious person organize a secular funeral? Can a secular person, with integrity, be given a religious send-off?' It is an acute question and one that needs careful handling. Liturgy is not some dry and ivory tower matter. Liturgy touches emotions and theology in the most practical of ways which is the cause of dissatisfaction to many clergy who find the ASB completely irrelevant in many of the pastoral situations in which they are expected to minister.

5. SPECIAL OCCASIONS

The Church of England being established as it is, finds itself host for civic occasions. In some churches at Christmas it is not unknown to have 25 carol services as various organizations, linked to the town, desire to meet there. But it is not peculiar to the Anglican church because other churches will also, from time to time, find themselves being the hosts of civic occasions besides Carol Services.

But the Christmas cycle in particular is one where clergy sometimes find problems. The building is used totally as a meeting place and there is no invitation, or desire, for clergy of the parish to make any contribution. In some situations there is a glaring lack of Christian content. In terms of the integrity of church councils and ministers, the issue is whether the building is to be used as a meeting place or for Christian worship. The question would be quite clear were it to be another faith who desired to use the building, but where it is a Parent-Teachers' Association, a local school or charitable organization, then the distinction is perhaps not quite so easily made. Nonetheless, it can be argued that even the entry into the church building, to see what is on offer and to feel the ethos of that particular building, is an aid to Christian proclamation.

Then there are, of course, the civic occasions when the Mayor, having been duly elected, desires to hold his inaugural service in the church, or perhaps to hold it near the end of his year of service as a thanksgiving. The civic service gives opportunity for somebody to proclaim the Christian gospel within the context of civic responsibility. But what of lesson readers from another faith reading their scriptures; or a sect member reading the Bible? What if the Mayor is a Muslim or a Hindu, a non-Christian or a rogue? Can we, with integrity, allow the church building to be used in this way?

Remembrance Day services and the hymns in particular can be points of conflict. The Remembrance Day hymns seem to suggest that those who died in the war have in fact made a sacrifice equivalent to that of our Lord and Saviour, Jesus Christ and to suggest that the hymn should be excluded and another substituted is an immediate confrontation! Truths and integrity, sentimentalism and memory, all meet in a rich cauldron.

The Church of England has had a glorious history and, Barchester Towers as well as television, Dave Allen and Derek Nimmo notwithstanding, has presented a picture of life in the nation with its links to the church in attractive, as well as unattractive, modes. Because of the established nature of the Church of England and the way in which the context and culture of our country has changed, we know that at the present time, questions are being raised about the establishment of the church. The Archbishop of York has raised questions about the Coronation Oath when the time comes for a new monarch and Simon Hughes, Liberal Democrat M.P. for Bermondsey, has attempted to raise the question in Parliament. But for all these special occasions there will be Christians present who on Sunday regularly worship with a local church. Those people, the lay members of the church, face questions of integrity as they face the general public and give answers for their faith and its implications. The recent problems in Gloucester illustrate this through the experience of Christians in their work place, besides the hurt felt by clergy in their profession inside and outside that diocese.

In some situations the social implications of the gospel raise issues. People who (perhaps more so in the past than now) attended church because it was a socially acceptable thing to do. There have always been the jokes which said the Church of England was the Tory party at prayer, or it was the place for ladies to show off their new hats; but life has changed and the degree to which our country is Christian has declined, so that there is a greater distinction now between those who believe and those who do not believe. Of course there are still those who go to church out of custom and tradition but perhaps the social set is not quite as dominant as it might once have been perceived to be.

But there is also a problem when an eclectic group, an insider group, a spiritual group or one with a particular theological stance, high-jacks a whole church. It has been seen to take place over issues regarding Women's Ordination, Prayer Book Catholic situation, charismatic expression, or simply small power groups, like families who, wanting the church to go in a particular way, have either engineered or found themselves to be in the leading influential positions of leadership. When a church is high-jacked in such a way, the local church nature has been compromised and where a clergyman coming into a situation allows that to continue, surely his integrity is being challenged; but if he tries to do something about it, his life is likely to be hellish.

There are clergy who say that if the laity do not like the types of services that are being held they can go to another church. That is an exclusivism, which is surely alien to the gospel. When it happens in an urban setting the consequences may not be as intense as when it is implemented in a rural context but it is nonetheless changing ownership of the church from God to a group of people for their own ends.

There is then, of course, the whole area of money-raising. How right is it for the church to be seeking money from those outside the church congregation? We know, of course, that there are congregations who wish to avoid the painful cost of sacrifice to themselves and will always do as much as possible to get money from outsiders, or by renting out church premises. But there are in many localities people that we might call God fearers who may not be regular worshippers themselves but certainly have the interests of the church and of God at heart and who will gladly provide the resources to keep the show on the road. Again, problems arise when such gifts are given with strings attached. The old saying that 'he who pays the piper calls the tune' is a very real one in certain situations and the integrity of the gospel is at risk if it means that only certain pieces of work can be financed on a patronage/sponsorship basis.

Then of course in all congregations there are clock-watchers. People who will judge how good a service has been according to how precise the 'one hour for God' slot has been observed. How often do we hear comments about a good sermon being short!? How often do we hear complaints about hymns having verses omitted? How often do we hear people saying that they cannot stay for after church fellowship because they have to get home in order to deal with the Sunday lunch? All these matters, in the eyes of eternity, are of little significance but the reality is that many people wish to give God only a limited amount of time, rather than to take him on as full time. Clock watchers can bring pressure upon the clergy in a way in which they perhaps are not aware but which, nonetheless, affects the whole delivery of a clergyman's ministry.

To-day's moral climate is such that increasingly churches have members with little or no background knowledge upon which to build. It means that the teaching ministry of the church needs strengthening in many instances, but more importantly it means that assumptions cannot be made, even among the committed and Church Councils, about traditional values, as they have come to be called. Take for instance the whole question of people living together prior to marriage—an increasing custom. Or the long standing relationships which have never been formalised in a wedding ceremony where a partner is a Sunday School teacher, or even on the Church Council.

What of couples living together who begin confirmation preparation? Are they to live apart; delay confirmation until the marriage? Here in the pews morality and integrity touch more than the clergy person.

But then there is the liturgy itself. To what extent are clergy expected to be able to dot every I and cross every t as far as doctrinal statements are concerned? Don Cupitt remains a licensed clergyman within the Church of England, but there are those who find that fact hard to swallow! As far as the laity are concerned, how far is an agreement to all that the Creeds have to say a pre-requisite for membership or integrity within the congregation? After all, saying 'We believe in God . . .' as the ASB Rite A Creed now puts it, is surely a statement that that is what the church believes, not what I personally accept—or that is the way some look at it.

But even at the heart of our worship is prayer and intercession. Can the congregation always say with integrity the 'Amen' when the person leading has been praying for something they cannot agree with? Praying for or praying against the ordination of women might be one example, political prayers could be another. There are even some passages of scripture about which, when one is read as the lesson for the day, some find it hard to say 'This is the Word of the Lord'!

6. GOING FORWARD

Who is sufficient for these things? Clergy need support and fellowship; laity need to be trusted and taken into confidence. But integrity is costly. Truth does bring with it strange repercussions. The marriage applicant who returned with a conscience that he had not given the correct address, for example, faced the truth but it cost him a Special Licence! When Joseph, as the Genesis story records it, ran for his reputation refusing to compromise his integrity, he still carried the blame and the punishment! When Job suffered all that he did, he still believed in God. Integrity meant pain and misunderstanding and it is in this area, that clergy and lay people alike need to be able to share the confrontation and division and find common ground for agreement.

But in all this the question of accountability is relevant. To whom are ministers accountable? To God? To their congregation? To the Bishop? To people who make demands? To the spoken and unspoken expectations? Are they accountable to God, minister, one another or to their friends and neighbours who expect the church's ministry to be available when they want it? We can never minimize the pain that some lay members of our churches endure at the hand of family and friends and neighbours because of their loyalty to church congregation and minister.

Compromise is usually given a negative connotation but theologically can that be substantiated? What could be more compromising than the fact of God becoming human? The incarnation is in itself a compromise of God's glory but for a reason and a goal—that of the salvation of the world. In many of the issues raised during this discussion, finding a solution and way forward will involve compromise but that is not necessarily sinful.

In the first place, we need to ask: *How can we develop integrity?*

Popularity and peer-group pressure always affect judgments, and clergy are no more immune to it than church members. How many PCC or Synod members look to see how others are voting before raising their hand!

Increasingly, clergy and laity look to, or are expected to look to, the bishop who has become not only the focus for unity in a diocese but the centre of management and control. Hence clergy find themselves working out their integrity, not only with the pressures from public, the world and the laity, but also through the authority to which they acknowledged they gave their allegiance at ordination.

Integrity is not something which we can buy off the shelf; it comes out of our make-up, belief, value-systems and experience. There is something instinctive, as well as something learned.

'I never thought of it that way', is a response one hears in the course of a discussion. Integrity of action comes out of teaching and understanding of the issues involved. It derives from facts. Thus reflection and prayer lie behind our actions and reactions. Integrity is allied to our spirituality and discipleship, for a rogue whose behaviour cannot be trusted, is said to be lacking in integrity! Discipleship means living the new life in Christ, a life in fellowship with the light of Christ, not with the darkness of the world. Integrity will find itself fuelled through prayer, as we grow into Christ's likeness and develop his mind. Integrity is developed through spirituality.

The next thing to ask is: *How do we retain integrity?*

There are a number of things which come to mind here. We need to resist temptation; we need to discern the situation; we need to develop the ability to say 'no' with grace and we need to avoid being pushed into a corner and above all, we need to know ourselves.

A number of years ago I had the following experience when we had had the church completely re-cleaned and re-decorated. The contractor, who had sub-contracted much of the work out, came after completion and payment to check whether or not we were pleased with the work. He offered to decorate a room in the vicarage for every new job he got on my recommendation. I thanked him for the offer but said that whilst it was kind of him, I would not take up the offer but, of course, would still recommend his work. There are people who gladly and happily do things for the church and their goodwill is to be appreciated and cultivated but we need to discern when that goodwill is being used as a lever for a favour to bend the rules. Here we are pushed back on spiritual resources. Ultimately, it is always our walk with God that is important. We must constantly walk by the spirit, so that his gifts and grace at work in us provide that gift of discernment so necessary. Satan triumphs when the church, through the life of its clergy or lay people, is found wanting and in the whole arena of integrity, spiritual warfare cannot be ignored or belittled.

Discernment is the ability to see behind the obvious and interpret the true relevance of the facts as presented. It demands the objective interpretation of facts. Men of the road really can tell good stories and their grapevine is very effective when a soft touch has been sourced. The ability to discern the facts, so often given after the DSS offices are closed for the day, or we are in a hurry and distracted by some other commitment, is so vital. The need to perceive for whose benefit a course of action is being followed is important. After all, the giving of money may not be in the best interest of the enquirer, only a let out for the giver who really wants to get on to the next engagement. This leads us on to the next practical matter.

No-one likes saying 'no' for it makes us feel guilty and there are people who play on that fact as they make demands upon the church and the clergy for their ministry.

To say 'no' to a request is never easy because our feelings do come in to things. Guilt; having our time and space interrupted; a half-truth catching a raw nerve. Whatever it might be, we are disturbed; our equilibrium is shattered and our judgment is clouded.

The ability to say 'no' in a positive way, therefore, is important. Give a reason for taking one course of action rather than another; point out why it might be better to follow a different course of action than the one desired. Thus Jesus declined the request for James and John to be given the best seats in the kingdom of heaven and he did so in a positive way by pointing to God only as being the one who could do that (Mark 10.35-45).

Problems always arise when we allow ourselves to be trapped in a corner and as trapped animals bite and lash out, so humans do the same. Anger with ourselves at being stupid; not seeing what was happening; not having the right answer; not being on our guard. The ability to stay objective is vital. Reflection and constant prayer will help us to keep us on our toes, especially if we have to face the ultimate truth regarding integrity, which is *that of knowing ourselves.*

When Joseph as Genesis records the story, ran for his reputation away from Potiphar's wife, he still carried the blame and punishment! When Job suffered all that he did, he still believed God. At times integrity will call for pain and misunderstandings and here lay persons and clergy alike need to be able to share and support one another over confrontation and division. Knowledge of self and of one another eases the stress caused.

And this is where support groups are helpful; where pastoral support is necessary and where guided reflection brings insight. Some make use of diarising and journaling methods to assist, but often it is the more direct contact and discussion which is needed. Prayer support and shared fellowship within and outside parish structures are needed.

It is being increasingly realized that self-knowledge, arising from God's knowledge, is important. The Myers-Briggs Type Indicator helps to a certain degree for we are then able to recognize why we act in certain ways, according to our type. But ultimately, it is the shadow part of us which needs sanctifying for from the cellar, come the reactions which determine our integrity. Integrity is linked with spirituality, theology, knowledge, personality and with sanctification. Carlos Valles says:

'We too stand before ourselves in a double-faced attitude. We love ourselves, as we undoubtedly do, in our own interest and out of our very first self-preservation instinct; and at the same time, in diverse aspects and in diverse ways, we also hate ourselves, as our experience simply shows and our memory testifies. And there is nothing wrong with it. On the contrary, we may have already experienced how our relationships with others improve when we know and accept the fact that they have always been, and will continue to be, love-hate relationships'[1]

Integrity, in relationship to worship, seems to touch at the very heart of the love-hate dilemma. Loving God, loving self, loving neighbour, loving truth, loving to draw others into the kingdom and at the same time, hating God for the cost sometimes involved; ourselves for the guilt we feel at saying 'no'; our neighbour for daring to make the demand on us; truth that it gets us into these dilemmas. But ultimately, the path of sanctification is one of God's spirit at work in us and he is the one who is present in all worship situations and in all the demands which they precipitate. By his grace at work in us we have inner peace and despite the fact that integrity brings opposition by it we win respect. May God give us all the integrity possible for our day by day living.

[1] Carlos Valles, *I love you, I hate you,* p.114.

APPENDIX: FOR LENT OR HOUSE GROUP STUDY

(Allow 90 minutes for each session outside any time for refreshments before of after)

Week 1
Starters. Allow up to 20 minutes to introduce each other by:

asking each person to state 4 things about themselves which are important to them including their feelings about their name.

Then invite the group to respond to the following statements:
'The world isn't like it used to be'
'You used to be able to go out and leave your door unlocked.'
'You don't know whom you can trust these days.'

List the key points made.
. . . .

Say a prayer asking for the guidance of the Holy Spirit
. . . .

Look at Nehemiah chapter 7
Why was Hanani chosen to be in charge?
In what ways does the fear of God affect us to-day?

What difference in lifestyle is expected of clergy and ministers from that of the congregation?
. . . .

What do we learn from *Deuteronomy 9.5* about the relationship between God's blessings and our actions?

How would we define integrity?
. . . .

Discuss the following
'Your neighbour, a church member, tells you how s/he went to church at Christmas but was taken aback to see a known alcoholic and layabout there and overheard a request for a blessing of their new marriage'.

What issues are raised by such a scenario?
Who is affected?
. . . .

Draw the session to a close by reading Matt. 22.16, spending some time in silence reflecting on it.

Conclude with the Grace.

For next week: Ask people to think about what affects our integrity.

Week 2
Make a formal start with a prayer.

Open report back:
Invite people to share their thoughts from the week's reflection on 'The things that affect integrity'. (10 minutes).
. . . .

Now Look at Genesis 39 and discuss the cost of integrity for Joseph
. . . .

Discuss
'I cannot hear what you are saying because what you are shouts too loud at me'.
What is meant by the person who said this?
How does it affect me?

Now list the various types of service which are held in your church:
Having listed, explore 'What is the purpose of each?'.

Discuss: 'What is the relationship between what we do and what we say in a service?'. How important are symbolic actions? How can they be misunderstood?
. . . .

'For whom are services held in church?' List the various possibilities.

In what ways could the integrity of a congregation be compromised?

Close with a time of prayer focusing on the life of the church.

MINISTERIAL INTEGRITY IN LITURGY

Week 3
Start this week's session by inviting group members to share any experience they have had recently over the cost of holding their integrity and the temptation to be dishonest in some way. (Allow 15 minutes)

Read Acts 2.36-end
i. What do we learn about life in the early church from this passage?
ii. If baptism involves repentance, on what basis do we baptize children?
iii. 'Those who were being saved' (v.47)—What is meant by that phrase?

Spend time in silent reflection on the passage and the issues raised (5 minutes).

Questions for Discussion
a. What do members of the congregation think as to when baptisms should take place in the life of the Church?
b. 'I turn to Christ'. 'I repent of my sins'. 'I renounce evil'. Who can make these statements?
c. Who qualifies for having their baby baptized? Do parents have to be married? Of what importance is the local Church?
d. What part does Folk Religion play in the desire for babies to be Christened? Discuss a policy for the baptism of infants in your church and agree three main points.

Close with prayer for homes and family life.

Week 4
Depute two people in the group to be James and John, the rest to be the disciples.

Read Mark 10.35-45

Give opportunity for 'James and John' and 'the disciples' to look at the passage and talk with one another about it.

Get the group to be 'in role' and for James and John and the disciples to discuss the issues raised by this incident.

Note feelings and important points made.

Introduce the question of the church and its responsibilities over marriage. Read the Introduction to the marriage service.

Raise the following issues for discussion:
1. Who should the church allow to marry in the church?
2. Why do people want a church wedding?
3. If people are divorced how should a decision be made as to whether or not they can re-marry in the church?
4. Why do 'the public' expect the church to fall in with their wishes?
5. Look at Mark 10.45. To what extent is the church to be servant and how can it avoid being doormat?
6. Why are we made to feel guilty if we say 'no'?

Time of devotion:
Start with a reflection on the relationship between prayer and integrity. Close with time of prayer;
for those soon to be married
for the preparation they will receive
for the clergy.

FOR NEXT WEEK:
Ask group members to come prepared with issues relating to the church, the congregation, funerals, memorials and their neighbours.

Provide the evaluation sheet to be handed out this week and returned next session.